# What Color?

### Sandra Sarsha
### Illustrated by Bob Masheris
### Photographed by Bill Burlingham

Rigby • Steck-Vaughn

www.HarcourtAchieve.com
1.800.531.5015

  What color can we paint the fence?

I like red.

I like blue.

I like green.

I like yellow.

I like purple.

I like orange.

We like all the colors.

We can use them all!

16